AF615062

JAMES FORD BELL AND HIS BOOKS

JAMES FORD BELL AND HIS BOOKS

THE NUCLEUS OF A LIBRARY

1993

ASSOCIATES OF THE JAMES FORD BELL LIBRARY

ISBN NUMBER 0-9601798-3-6

PUBLISHED BY THE ASSOCIATES OF THE JAMES FORD BELL LIBRARY,
UNIVERSITY OF MINNESOTA, 472 WILSON LIBRARY, 309 19TH AVENUE
SOUTH, MINNEAPOLIS, MINNESOTA 55455.

Foreword

ON October 30, 1953, James Ford Bell presented his collection of rare books to the University of Minnesota. The dedication ceremonies included a program of papers which were published by the University of Minnesota Press in 1954 as *Book Collecting and Scholarship*. This early book contains essays by Theodore C. Blegen, Stanley Pargellis, Colton Storm, and Louis B. Wright, in addition to the commentary titled "Bound Fragments of Time" by Mr. Bell. The latter is reprinted in the present book, with the permission of the University of Minnesota Press. The collection in 1953 consisted of about 600 books. The new Curator, John Parker, was in the audience for the dedication. From that time until Mr. Bell's death in 1961, these two men built the Library together and determined its scope. Over the forty years since that time it has grown to over 15,000 titles, plus manuscripts and maps. The Library's subject is the Expansion of Europe, 1400 to 1800.

Mr. Bell expressed the hope that an organization would be formed to publicize and support the Library and its programs. In December, 1963 a group known as the Associates of the James Ford Bell Library was incorporated, and this organization has had a major role in the development of the Library. The Associates are publishing the present book as a celebration of the forty years that the James Ford Bell Library has been at the University. The main text of the book is from Mr. Bell himself, with selections from his diaries and correspondence relating to his books as well as the essay noted above. These writings from James Ford Bell give the reader an insight into his plans and hopes for the collection. He said of his Library, "What I have collected has been carefully chosen and is, I think, of a quality and an extent to form at least the nucleus of a library which...may someday take its place with others both in its extent and in the values it offers." Over the span of forty years the Library has grown and is productive. It has been the source of learning for many students, and a place of joy for researchers. This success is made possible by support from the Associates, the Bell Family, the James Ford Bell Foundation, and the University of Minnesota.

In this book, Dr. John (Jack) Parker provides a chapter on the development of the Library and its focus. Other contributions are by Mr. Charles H. Bell, son of James Ford Bell, Dr. Edward B. Stanford, Director of Libraries in 1953, and Mr. Brad Oftelie, Assistant Curator of the Library.

The Associates have been supportive of this publication, in particular the Directors, Elizabeth Z. Savage, President, William P. Laird, Treasurer, Rutherford Aris, Ford W. Bell, Judith Anderson Brindley, Charles Hann, Maynard B. Hasselquist, Irving B. Kreidberg, Melva Lind, Bernadette

Pyter Muck, Diane Neimann, John Parker, Curtis L. Roy, Mrs. Robert J. Schweitzer, Jr., and William A. Urseth. Irv Kreidberg worked with the design of the book. Brian Hanson typed all of the text on the computer, carefully and swiftly. We were assisted in consulting the diaries by Diane Neimann, Executive Director of the James Ford Bell Foundation, and staff members Miriam Nevala and Anne Krepski. The University Archives, courtesy of Penny Krosch, Archivist, lent us some of the early archival materials relating to the Library, which was much appreciated. Ms. Jean Toll, Archivist at General Mills, provided reference assistance. Mr. Charles H. Bell, Ms. Diane Neimann, and Ms. Jessie Richardson gave the manuscript careful readings and offered helpful suggestions. The James Ford Bell Foundation's grant to the Associates to assist with the cost of publication is deeply appreciated.

Carol Urness, Curator

Table of Contents

Charles H. Bell 

A Letter

DEAR Carol:

Unfortunately, during those early years when Father was striving to build his trade library, I seem to have very few recollections. However, it was always clear that he felt that one of the key fingerprints in the history of civilization and man was trade. Trade and trade routes, if carefully documented and preserved, in his opinion, would more clearly show the evolution of mankind than any other medium.

That concept was what motivated him in his enthusiasm for creating the trade library. In his early collecting periods he kept his findings in his home at Belford in Wayzata. At some point he had a two-story vault built inside the structure of his home, with the only entrance off of his den or study on the main floor in the southwest corner with a narrow iron staircase leading down to the lower basement floor.

I recall that he used rather extensively a rare book store in New York City to help him search out items that would fit his objectives, but he also made numerable trips in this country and abroad seeking out various treasured items or following up on leads which had been brought to his attention. Later, of course, he was so admirably assisted by John Parker.

It always seemed that the excitement of the search itself was stimulating but, of course, the finding of some new rare information which would shed light on the history and progress of civilization was a tremendous source of satisfaction.

He was certainly proud and pleased to have the Library become part of the University of Minnesota, where he served as a Regent for many years, but he would have been doubly proud of what John Parker and you have accomplished since his death in 1961.

A salute to you both. Best regards.

Charlie

Brad Oftelie

James Ford Bell

JAMES Ford Bell was born on August 16, 1879 in Philadelphia and came to Minneapolis with his parents in 1888. William Hood Dunwoody, a vice-president of Washburn Crosby Company, recruited James Stroud Bell, James Ford's father, to help rescue his company from growing competition and other economic difficulties associated with flour milling in the late nineteenth century. Young James attended Lawrenceville School in New Jersey. In 1901 he graduated with a degree in chemistry from the University of Minnesota. While still at the University, Mr. Bell set up a flour testing laboratory in his father's company, one of the earliest if not the first such laboratory in a flour mill. He went to work for Washburn Crosby as a salesman and was assigned Michigan as his territory. The towns were small. He saw a new one every day traveling by train, and the conditions were at times primitive. But the experience was invaluable. This was important to Mr. Bell because he believed in understanding all aspects of a business or any other endeavor, from the inside out. Selling his father's flour gave him an appreciation for those allied businesses involved with the product of wheat. He came to see that the miller was linked to the baker as well as to the farmer.

In 1902 Mr. Bell married Louise Heffelfinger. They had four children: James Ford, Jr., Charles, Samuel and Sally (Mrs. H.O. Perry).

Mr. Bell became a vice-president of Washburn Crosby in 1915. These were troubled times in Europe with the devastating war that eventually involved the United States. But the war also presented opportunities for American farmers and millers. As chairman of the Millers Committee in Minneapolis, Mr. Bell assumed a leadership role. In June 1917 Herbert Hoover, President Wilson's Director of the United States Food Administration, chose Mr. Bell to run the Administration's Milling Division. Members of the Division determined the price of wheat, bought wheat for the army and distributed free advice to millers concerning the different ways flour needed to be made from different grains in order to meet the demand. Later, with Mr. Hoover, Mr. Bell traveled to Europe to see firsthand the war's effect, especially in relation to European food production. Writing to Dr. John E. Bushnell of Westminster Church in Minneapolis in 1918, Mr. Bell comments, "Of one thing I am certain ... that until you have actually come into personal touch with the European situation, you cannot appreciate what a tremendous picture it has been and how hard to grasp, even when it has been presented with all details; nor can you realize the degree of suffering, self-sacrifice and grief patiently endured by the people of these war torn countries during the past four years." (This and other quotations below are from Mr. Bell's correspondence on deposit in the Minnesota Historical Society. The assistance provided by MHS is deeply appreciated.)

When the war ended Mr. Bell quickly left government service and returned to his company. He helped with the reorganization of Washburn Crosby and in 1925 became its president. The decade of the 1920s was a difficult one for farmers, including wheat farmers. Consumption had fallen off during the war and was not rising back upward. Farmers, encouraged by war needs, had increased production. The price for wheat fell. A plan to withhold grain from the market did not help and many farmers lost their land. Mr. Bell's solution to the problem was twofold: reduce the production of wheat, and encourage consumption. Regarding the latter he threw himself into his campaign "Eat More Wheat," complete with billboard and radio advertising. It was at this time that Mr. Bell began thinking about, as he saw it, the close relationship between the farmer and the miller. He recognized that the relationship was at times strained. For example, he wrote in a letter to Frank F. Henry of Washburn Crosby that "We hear an awful lot about how to do good farming, but the business man knows nothing about that, nor is his advice worth a two-penny bit. However, when it comes to the broader phases of the situation, the farmer does not want the business man's advice." Mr. Bell believed that in order to be successful each side must listen to and understand the other. He did not support any kind of price controls, believing them to be short-sighted. His faith in governmental policy was grounded in his Republican Party roots. Writing from Washington, D.C. to his Uncle, Samuel Bell, Jr. of Philadelphia, Mr. Bell states, "A good deal of agitation here on the different agricultural measures before Congress. There are so many of them and such a conflict of ideas and thought and personalities that the best course is to forget all about them." He summed up his approach to the economic troubles of the 1920s and 1930s in a letter to M.S. Rukeyser, financial editor of the *New York Evening Journal,* explaining, "I don't know of any other method than a simple and orderly procedure based on good sound economic principles." In 1928 he put those sound principles together in the formation of General Mills.

Mr. Bell consolidated four companies with his own to form General Mills. They were the Sperry Flour Company of the Pacific coast, the Kell group of mills in Oklahoma and Texas, the Red Star Milling Company of Kansas, and the Larrowe Milling Company of Michigan. As President of General Mills, Mr. Bell stressed research and technological developments in the new company, setting up kitchens for developing new products. The Mechanical Development Department, devoted to new tools and machines, was established in 1939. In 1942 it became the Mechanical Division. The Company grew quickly and steadily. In 1934 Mr. Bell became Chairman of the Board of Directors of General Mills. He was to serve in that capacity until 1947.

The Great Depression found Mr. Bell struggling with food production policies and in 1931 he became a member of President Hoover's Advisory Committee on Relief for

Unemployment. In December of that year an article by Mr. Bell appeared in the *Saturday Evening Post.* Its title was "The Public Attitude Toward Agriculture" and it dealt with the main problem surrounding agriculture, as Mr. Bell saw it, an abundant surplus. The problem was exacerbated by the government's purchase of the surplus. In the article Mr. Bell proposed the formation of a Federal Farm Reserve which would buy up agricultural land, beginning with marginal lands, to discourage overproduction. In the future, as the population increased, the Reserve would sell land to be put back into agricultural production. For the most part Mr. Bell's article received kind approval from a variety of people and organizations. He thanked them all and answered his critics as well. A lawyer from northwestern Minnesota, who represented many farmers, wrote Mr. Bell a rather caustic letter stating that the real problem in agriculture is the rich city businessmen who do not understand nor care about what it takes, day by day, to be a successful farmer. Mr. Bell met the criticism head on with clear thinking and humor and extended an offer of friendship. As the two corresponded a friendship did develop.

Mr. Bell eventually left the running of the corporation to others and dedicated more time to his other interests. His support for natural history was demonstrated at the Museum of Natural History at the University of Minnesota. His interest in the preservation of wildlife manifested itself in the creation of the Delta Waterfowl Research Station in Manitoba, Canada. He served as a Regent for the University of Minnesota. And he gave more time to his book collection.

Mr. Bell, in an effort to understand the flour milling business and how Minneapolis became such a center of flour milling, had collected books that dealt with the commerce of the Minnesota region. This had led him to the beaver trade and to the annual reports of French Jesuits, which were rich in detail of North American life as these early Europeans recorded it. Most of the books he gave to the University of Minnesota in October, 1953 were *Jesuit Relations* and other Americana.

Excerpts from Diaries and Correspondence

NOTE: Mr. Bell kept diaries for many years, commenting about events in his business and family life. From these diaries some selections relating to his association with the University of Minnesota have been selected for publication here. In his early diaries there are few comments about his book collecting. He mentions the books and their disposition more frequently in the 1940s. But Mr. Bell was an avid book collector from at least 1920. This is indicated in correspondence held at the University of Minnesota Archives, from which other selections are printed in the present book. The most fascinating files in the University Archives are those titled simply "Marco Polo" or "Pigafetta." These show the research that was done in relation to books and subjects of interest to Mr. Bell. His correspondence with the book dealers show what a discriminating book collector he became. Mr. Bell clearly enjoyed buying books and learning about them. He invested much time and energy in his collection.

In addition, Mr. Bell kept records of the date of purchase, the dealer and price for most of his books. This was important as he was preparing to transfer his collection to the University. In the following selections the additions in parentheses have been supplied by Charles H. Bell or Carol Urness. (CU)

Introduction

When the *Olympic* sailed from New York for England on March 7, 1925, America's most flamboyant and successful book dealer, Abraham Simon Rosenbach, was a passenger on the ship. Rosenbach had recently purchased the collection of Frederick K. Trowbridge, one of the founders of the Grolier Club. Mr. James Ford Bell, a miller and merchant from Minneapolis who was already a serious book collector, was also on board. The first recorded purchase from Rosenbach by Mr. Bell was *A Short State of the Countries and Trade of North America*, London, 1749, a pamphlet which is a nasty criticism of the Hudson Bay Company's monopoly on trade. Mr. Bell got it from Dr. Rosenbach in 1921, at a price of $40.00. No doubt the two enjoyed talking books, and the result is evident in a notebook titled "Book Prices, James F. Bell, 1925/1940." The entries are: "1925. Shakespeare 'Folios' $45,000.00—Rosenbach. Canterbury Tales—$7,500.00—Rosenbach"

In 1926 Mr. Bell bought the 1483 Caxton printing of John Gower's *Confessio Amantis* from Dr. Rosenbach for $13,500.00, also from the Trowbridge collection. James

Ford Bell had very quickly obtained some books of the highest literary value. The next year he received a research inquiry about his Shakespeare folios from a scholar in the English Department at Lehigh University. Also, under the binding of his *Confessio Amantis*, some pieces of a previously unknown Caxton Indulgence of 1481 were discovered. The writer of a short notice about this discovery called it "one of the greatest typographical 'finds' of the generation." Emphasis on the literary side of collecting did not eclipse his interest in history, for in 1926 Mr. Bell also purchased Walter Bigges, *A Summarie and True Discourse of Sir Frances Drakes West Indian Voyage*, London, Richard Field, 1598, at a price of $10,500.00.

This focus on trade, travel, and missionary reports, the developing ideas of geography, of encounters between different peoples was reflected in books he had purchased earlier. In 1921 he bought seven books from James F. Drake, including a copy of the Bigges account of Sir Francis Drake's expedition in its first Latin edition, 1588, at a price of $60.00. That was a "bargain" then, but the copy lacks the maps, which is why the James Ford Bell Library now has two copies of this work, the "bargain" and a complete one. Mr. Bell quickly learned to insist on completeness and fine condition in his book collecting. Mr. Bell purchased books in 1921 from George M. Chandler, Peter A. Porter, George D. Smith, Henry Sotheran, Grafton & Co., Lathrop Harper. His major acquisition was Richard Hakluyt's *Principall Navigations*, London, 1589, which he got from Brentano's for $725. As the years passed he continued to select

"Americana" steadily. The collection grew in importance and Mr. Bell's knowledge of book collecting and of his books developed as well. (CU)

1926 Diary.

Saturday, February 13th. Talked with H. (Herschel) V. Jones re purchase of Gutenberg Bible as a memorial to father. He talked to Rosenbach over the phone ...

Sept. 8, 1926 Personal note: Mr. Sickle here today and left for my inspection Kilmarnock Burns (1786), 1st edition Edinburgh and 1st edition London. Also 1st Beaumont & Fletcher (1647). He has given me an option on ten items of Eugene Field at $5000.

For thirteen years afterward there are no entries concerning book collecting in his diaries. The notebook cited above, though, lists book purchases for every year: for 1927 there is only one entry, but a most significant one, for it reads: "Jesuit Relations, $18,500.00 from Rosenbach." Other entries in the notebook show that Mr. Bell was buying books from Maggs Bros., and from Henry Stevens Son & Stiles, in addition to Rosenbach. His emphasis in his collecting was on Americana, and particularly on the North American accounts by the Jesuits. He got the 1613 edition of Samuel de Champlain's *Voyages* in 1928 and the 1632 edition in 1930. And his collection of *Jesuit Relations* kept growing remarkably. But he obviously simply liked nice books as well, and in 1932 he bought Robert Louis Stevenson's *A Child's Garden of Verses* with the Kate Greenaway illustrations. In 1934 he purchased a copy of the 1493 *Nuremberg Chronicle* at a price of $300.00 from Powers Department

Store in Minneapolis. The buyer for the book department there was J. Harold Kittleson, a faithful member of the Associates. Harold remembers carrying the book down the street to Mr. Bell's office!

Mr. Bell obtained the first English edition of Marco Polo's *Travels*, 1579, at a price of $3,500.00 in 1934. The following year he purchased another spectacular book from Rosenbach, the Columbus *Letter* of 1493, for $8,000.00. He continued adding to the *Jesuit Relations*. He got another edition of the *Travels* of Marco Polo, a Columbus *Letter* of 1494, and the first edition of Sir John Mandeville's *Travels*, 1485, in 1938. (CU)

1939 Diary.

March 15: Saw Rosenbach regarding the Scott items. He wants to discuss with me possibility of purchasing the (Herschel V.) Jones collection. Executive Committee meeting of AT&T.

Aug 16. My sixtieth birthday.

Aug 17. This morning Carl Jones came in to see about his father's library. I would like to purchase it if I had the money and a proper price.

By the end of 1940 Mr. Bell had invested $185,438.78 in the 85 titles cited in the notebook. A memo from Miss Marguerite Guthrie dated May 15, 1953, indicates that these purchases "were entered in your old account books as investments." The titles in the notebook represent only a portion of Mr. Bell's collecting, as is shown by the voluminous correspondence that he had with book dealers. Many of the early books that he purchased are not included in the notebook. The amount of research involved in the evaluations of books offered is an insight into his standards as a book collector, which were peerless. In order to understand the books more completely, he obtained bibliographies and reference books. By the 1940s he had a small but outstanding collection, with great strength in the *Jesuit Relations* and in other books about North America. Mr. Bell had come to the point in his life when he was thinking about the future of the collection. It was in this same year that he became a member of the Board of Regents of the University of Minnesota, his alma mater. In the diaries his interests in the Board, the Museum of Natural History—later named the James Ford Bell Museum of Natural History, and his books are mentioned more prominently. (CU)

1940 Diary.
January 12. Regents' meeting.
Jan. 19. A.M.: Saw Frank Chapman Andrews at American Museum of Natural History. Secured their consent to release (Francis Lee) Jacques to paint some backgrounds for our museum.
Feb.14, Regents. It appears to me we are just doing clerical work, nothing with an education or cultural side. I have asked if this cannot be enlarged upon.
Oct. 5. (Regents). One member of the Board tells me he has been there 17 years and this is the first time the Board has been anything but a rubber stamp. He seems delighted with the new order.

1942 Diary.

Jan. 9—All day meeting of Board. Visited the School of Mines. Saw the experiments in separating iron and taconite, both the magnetic and non-magnetic types. The Board is inquiring into the untrodden highways and byways of the university, to their edification and education ....

Sept. 11. (Regents). A busy session. We will streamline education; make it continuous and direct its objectives to war contributions, such as mathematics, physics, trigonometry, drawing, English. This should bring about reforms which I hope will be of permanent character. A change from four years of campus club life to intensive effort on fundamentals, with extended courses for those requiring more comprehensive work ...

Sept. 24, 1942. Talked with President (Walter C.) Coffey in respect to increasing the services of the university to supplement manpower with womanpower. I find that this has ready acceptance.

Nov. 30. Later I suggested to Coffey that we include in the University Budget a revolving fund of $50,000 for aid of students who, by reason of the elimination of summer vacations are no longer able to earn their way. 68% of the men at the University earn their way either wholly or in substantial part.

1943 Diary.

November 1. Mr. (Frank K.) Walter, the former librarian of the University came in to look over the books. I am hopeful he can finish the cataloging which Miss (Bertha) Berg (Jespersen) was unable to complete.

1944 Diary.

Jan. 4. Mr. Walter was in this afternoon. We have gone over the work he is doing in connection with the books. He seems to find a great deal of material of interest. I am still torn between my ideas of what disposition to make of these, whether to give them to the University as the nucleus of a library or to put them under the hammer that other collectors may enjoy them as I have. Once in a library, they remain. The returns to my estate in either case would be about the same.

Feb. 10. Mr. Walter was in during the afternoon and we talked over the matter of the catalog of the books. I find him an interesting and delightful gentleman.

Nov. 29, 1944. Dr. Walter was in and we went over the proposed acquisition. The Waldseemueller proves to be the third edition and not the first, as represented. We are returning it ... (This refers to the *Cosmographiae introductio*, rather than to the famous gore map which Mr. Bell acquired much later).

1947 Diary.

June 9, 1947. Dean (Richard) Kozelka (University of Minnesota) came in to see me today with two other gentlemen; advised that I had been awarded membership in some honorary society. I do not know what this is all about but apparently I have to "sing for my supper" with a speech on August 27.

1948 Diary.

Jan. 14. Dr. (Errett W.) McDiarmid was in this morning. We reviewed the Rives catalog, to be sold at the Parke Bernet

Galleries next Monday. I see nothing here of particular interest. Largely Latin America, and apart from our field.... I met Mr. Henry C. Taylor while at Norias last week. He has asked me to dinner that night and to attend the auction. He has quite a comprehensive collection, but more in the fields south of what we intend to cover.

October 4: (Regents) ... I concluded my remarks by the suggestion that we take steps within a reasonable time to formalize the gift of my Americana library, following out my intention to give them custody over a period of ten years after which, if they have made notable additions, it should come to them as a gift; otherwise the trustees should have the right to give it to some other institution where it will receive proper recognition and expansion. It occurs to me however that I might add another clause, to the effect that if they fail to carry out the terms, the trustees should be given the option of disposing of the library under the hammer and using the proceeds for the expansion of the natural history museum that it might embrace the broader field of all natural science.

1949 Diary.

August 16, 1949. (JFB 70th birthday). I had hoped this anniversary was going to pass without notice or comment. However, having reached the Biblical score of years, one's thoughts turn to whether he has lived too long, or whether the remaining time and one's mentality will be sufficient to meet the hopes of the future in the days that remain. I have had a barrage of letters, wires, flowers, etc. It is all very warming and brings back a flood of memories.

1950 Diary.

8 May 1950. President (James Lewis) Morrill of the University came in with a copy of the catalog. (This is the *Jesuit Relations and Other Americana in the Library of James F. Bell*, compiled by Frank K. Walter and Virginia Doneghy, published by the University of Minnesota Press.) Discussed the announcement of the publication of the book. Have been worried about the extent of the publicity. I would like to have gotten this through without it, but the University has done so much that I assume I shall have to accede to their wishes. Had Charlie Bell in as one of the trustees under the will.

November 17: With President Morrill, Dean (Malcolm M.) Willey and Mr. McDiarmid looked over the possibilities of a "Treasure Room" at the library. I have asked that they consult a good architect both for the location of sites and to engage all arrangements.

December 30, 1950. This is my last day in my present offices in the company's building. It marks another milestone in my business career. A further parting of that relationship which I have maintained over all the years of my active business life and to which I have given all the ability that I possessed. In a measure, I feel like the pilot who has brought the ship out to open sea and who is now going down over the side, waving Godspeed and a pleasant voyage. - The new year will see me in the new quarters across the way. It is hard to go. But it is the right thing to do, and believing it is the right, I shall find happiness in it.

1951 Diary.

March 30. Mr. McDiarmid and Mr. (Winston) Close (architect) of the University were here regarding the Treasure Room. I have outlined my ideas and hope his next sketches will be something along the line I have in mind.... I signed the trust agreement in regard to the library.... We are still having snow.

May 25, 1951. Received by action of the Board the Distinguished Achievement Award of the University. The University does not grant honorary degrees except to the academic staff, which is proper. Therefore, this comes as signal recognition. It is certainly very gratifying. - Attended a class luncheon. About 30 present. This is my 50th anniversary. I have passed through fifty years, three wars, and all the economic and social disturbances incident to these and the changing world. I think I have done my duty.

August 8. Mr. McDiarmid, who now succeeds to the head of the College of S. L. A. (Science, Literature and Arts), brought in Dr. (Edward B.) Stanford, who is acting librarian.... He also brought in Mr. Close, the University architect, who is drawing up designs for the Treasure Room. They have worked out two very good locations, but I am not at all in sympathy with the monotonous type of panelling which he has incorporated in his sketches.

1952 Diary.

March 18: (New York) I met with Mr. Close of the University and we spent the day visiting various art dealers looking for material and ideas for the book room which I am planning to build at the University Library at Minneapolis....

Called on Mr. (Roland) Tree. He tells me the (J.C.) McCoy collection is here in this country and while there is no money involved, they will make the books available to him for disposal as needed. Tree suggested that when he is ready he would like to have Miss (Virginia) Doneghy come on for a few days, to be followed by myself. (The catalog of McCoy's collection, *Canadiana and French Americana*, was published in 1931, and Mr. McCoy gave Mr. Bell a copy of the catalog in Europe in 1932.)

April 7: (New York) Concluded the book deals with Mr. Tree. Talked with Henry Taylor and found him rather provoked that he had not had first, or equal, chance at the selecting of books from the McCoy Library, but he ignores the fact that we had a long correspondence with McCoy and had asked for the privilege of a first opportunity in case they were disposed of.

September 3: I have been going over some of the material which has come from John Carter Brown Library. One grows envious of that period when so much material was available and could be secured at prices which seem fantastically low as compared with today, when the supply is so small it is rather discouraging to try to get together enough material of comprehensive scope.... In a memorandum to the (University of Minnesota) trustees of the book trust I have outlined some suggestions in case the books are transferred to the University as I hope: (1) The collection should be housed in separate quarters; (2) it should be under the direction of an advisory group selected by the President, either within or without the University as may be deemed of service to the collection; (3) the university should designate as a part of the library all the collateral works they now possess which would be of interest with it; (4) they should promote the idea, either through the special trustees or through the library itself of forming a group of "associates of the library"; (similar to The Associates of the John Carter Brown Library, etc.), through whom it is hoped contributions might be made and new items acquired; (5) there is no objection to extending the scope of the library if that is thought desirable. It should be limited to those items which fall into a selected period, say, not beyond the beginning of the 19th century.... I think I shall have to make some effort to expand the field, or at least of including supporting items in the way of maps or material of the pre-discovery period showing the forces which led to expansion and discovery.

November 7: Mr. (William T., University News Service) Harris and Dr. Stanford were in about the book room at the University. We decided merely to mention the room as a housing for rare books and make no announcement of the library until the opening.

November 22: (Saturday) Miss (Annabelle) Johnson, Miss (Virginia) Doneghy, Mr. (Harold) Russell and Mr. (James) Kingsley were out looking over the books in the library which might be desirable to add to the University gift.

1953 Diary.

March 17, 1953. New York. Looked over some items at (H.P.) Kraus's (rare) book shop.

April 21: Dr. Stanford and Mr. Parker, who is candidate for the curatorship of the collection, were in, together with Miss

Doneghy. We had a discussion of the work of getting the library together. I am very favorably impressed with Mr. Parker.... I am attending the meeting of the Friends of the Library tonight.

April 29, 1953. Mr. (H.P.) Kraus was here from New York and we have been inspecting the books. Inasmuch as we have several items obtained before my determination on the field of Americana, which therefore do not fit in the present scheme of the collection, these should be disposed of and the proceeds used for the acquisition of items appropriate to the Americana collection.

May 14: Visited the library. Dr. Stanford and I looked over the books now on approval. The room is beginning to shape up now, with the ceiling approaching final stages.

August 4: Spent the morning with Robert Samuels at the University looking over the new book room, which I think on the whole is satisfactory after we have made certain changes ironing out some of the lack of individuality in the various pieces of furniture selected.

September 4: Mr. Parker was in this afternoon. We have merely discussed possibilities of building up some motive behind the book collection. We need to extend our contacts.

September 14: (New York) Saw Lathrop Harper; they had some interesting items. One particularly interesting item which I asked him to pass on to us for real study is supposedly the log of the pilot who took over the Magellan expedition on the death of Magellan. (This is the Pigafetta manuscript that eventually went to Yale University. Mr. Bell was very unhappy that he did not get this manuscript.)

October 1, 1953. To the Library in the morning to see about the furnishings of the room. I am very much pleased with the way Mr. Parker is taking hold of the curatorship.

October 28: I am busy checking up things at the University for the dedication of the room. Our trip to Des Moines, which is scheduled for tomorrow, has been called off until the first of the week, to accommodate C. H. B.... I am annoyed at French & Co. Despite their promises to have everything here for the opening of the room, they have failed to do so in several categories.

October 30, 1953. Today we dedicated the book room at the University and were privileged to have with us some eminent representatives from three great libraries as well as Mr. (Edward) Weeks of the Atlantic Monthly.

October 31: Dr. Stanford gave a very interesting talk on the functions of the library.

November 5: At the University in the morning for a little huddle on some of the new items being offered, particularly the Caxton. Asked Mr. Parker to dig out from the Morgan Library and the Huntington a fair evaluation of the item, pointing out that the book dealer is a very essential part in the field of books and is entitled to a reasonable remuneration for his services, but it is not in the interest of any book collector or library to feel we are the victim of gouging.

December 29: Mr. Parker came in and we have discussed his New York trip and the possibilities of purchasing the Waldseemueller gore map. He will proceed to New York and spend a little time visiting with Mr. Kraus and examining into the matter further. This represents a very substantial expense, although one which I feel will give distinguishment to the collection.

1954 Diary.

March 30: Spent the morning at the University with Mr. Parker going over some of the items they have purchased, as well as those we have purchased or have in contemplation. On the latter we came to decisions.

April 13: To the library this morning. Reviewed some of the new items. It is gratifying to note that of the desirable (to us) items in the Parke Bernet sale of Western Americana, the University has almost all.

April 14: I have been turning over in my own mind the suggestion that our library at the University develop documentation of this new era of discovery and expansion by airplane, the importance of which is only secondary to some of the great periods of history, particularly as it affects trade. This is so obvious it seems strange someone has not already thought of it, and it may be that, like many other obvious things, we have overlooked it. Had Dean (Malcolm) Willey, Cy Plattes, and Dick (T.R.) Anderson in to lunch. I find quick response, and enthusiastic, from Willey the same as I did yesterday when I outlined it to Stanford and Parker at the book room. This is all right as an idea, but it is only an idea. The next step is how to approach it. Someone must be found to devote his entire attention to working up all the information possible on what we want and how we should proceed to get it. Told Willey I would finance a reasonable amount in the preliminary steps. He felt if we could get things there set up in its true significance, we probably could get grants from the Ford Foundation, which is interested in this kind of thing. Anyhow, the thing is worthy of thought and consideration. We will gather a small group in the week of the twenty-sixth to discuss it further. I have suggested we include Dr. Morrill, Dean (Theodore) Blegen, Dean (Athelstan) Spilhaus, and maybe one or two others. A library of this kind, the material for which could be gathered together now at little cost, would be something of real worth and distinction. Its practicability, however, must be the determining factor.... Took night train to Chicago.

April 27: Mr. Parker comes in from the University telling me of an offer from (Lionel) Robinson in London of the manuscript map of 1424 from the Phillips Collection, which is of great importance and probably the first indication of the discovery of the Western Hemisphere. It would take precedence over the Waldseemueller. It is probably the earliest suggestion of such a discovery, which customarily would be concealed during that period. It sounds very interesting. (The 1424 nautical chart is by Zuane Pizzigano and is one of the outstanding items in the James Ford Bell Library).

May 10: We discussed at length the idea I advanced in respect to increasing the scope of the trade library beyond the realm of land and sea, to embrace air travel as well. In this respect the penetration of new lands with new trade is certainly of great significance. The initial material is still available, and if the problem is practical we could establish here in Minneapolis one of the great trade libraries of the world, particularly in this latter field where material would still be available by processes well within our reach.... I am not at all convinced that the magnitude of the thing is beyond us, but the question is: has it sufficient merit to warrant an investigation, the initial steps of which I am willing to finance. I do not think we would be interested in air travel merely as a matter of communication. It would be where the motivating idea was contact for trade that we would want to venture.... The whole idea seems to have sparked an enthusiastic response. Dean (Athelstan) Spilhaus has suggested that Mr. Lee of the CAA be invited to come out for a preliminary talk.... The consensus of opinion is that the idea is intriguing and well worth further exploration.

May 25: Mr. Parker came over and we discussed the matter of the Waldseemueller map which Mr. (Richard) Zinser left with us last Friday. This is an extremely important item, although I think the price is somewhat out of line. Mr. Parker will get hold of Mr. (Lawrence C.) Wroth of the John Carter Brown Library and see what his reactions are. (This map of 1507 is one of the most famous maps known and has been frequently reproduced in books of many kinds.)

June 2: I went over to the University and met with Dr. Morrill and Willey, Stanford, and Parker. The question was whether, in the purchase of the Waldseemueller map and the nautical map of 1424, in the whole library program we are attempting to do too much in an area which is not prepared by understanding to develop it in the future.

August 17: Jack Parker is back from Europe and we have had a very interesting review of his trip and the contacts he has made. There is notice here that Life Magazine will feature the Waldseemueller map and the Chart of 1424 in the

issue of October 11 and we shall have to plan to meet the volume of visitors who will follow as result of this publicity.
September 22: I am disappointed at the news Life will not publish the two maps as they had indicated. It is rather a discourteous act at this late date when, by withholding the information, we have lost several favorable opportunities to bring credit to the University. However, we have decided we should make no comment whatsoever, but seek other sources if they are open.
October 26: Lunched at the University as a guest of Mr. Stanford, to meet Mr. Lloyd Brown, the cartographer and author, who is speaking tonight on the anniversary of the dedication of the Bell Room. I find a kindred spirit in an appreciation of trade as an expression of living.
December 22: The library is getting an increasing number of inquiries from other institutions for material with which they can prepare their scholars.

1955 Diary.
May 13: At the University this morning; had a long talk with Parker, who is getting ready for his trip abroad, and with Dr. Stanford. We are all convinced we have been very wise in broadening the scope of the library under the caption of 'trade' rather than having it identified (as it might be) as purely Americana. We discussed various steps for publicity. The lines of approach seem excellent.
August 22: Went over to the University and had a satisfactory talk with Jack Parker. The amount of stuff that is piling in has put him rather behind. However, he assures me we have

an option which may go four or five years on much of the material.

September 10: Had a long talk with Mrs. Vera Bowman, the president of the Woman's Club, which is certainly a growing element in the city. She wanted me to fill one of their evening programs. I told her I was too old to undertake fixed engagements and the effort they involved. I suggested Mr. Parker, and this was agreed upon if he is willing, and with the understanding that if I happen to be in the city, and the spirit moves me, I will attend the meeting and introduce Mr. Parker but there was to be no fixed obligation on my part to do so—only if I happened to be here and the spirit moved, particularly the spirit!

October 17: Checked with Jack Parker about getting some slides for use in his book talks, particularly that at the Women's Club. Mr. Nasvik has kindly offered to cooperate. Dropped in to see them making slides of some of the choice items. I am delighted with the rapidity with which we have secured and added items to the library. Really there are some very fine things.

October 28: Jack Parker gave a talk on the books at the Woman's Club last night. The reactions were very good. I see no reason why we should not spread this further, to the added prestige of the University and the library.

1956 Diary.

March 14: Jack Parker was in this morning. We have been checking up on various items of interest and also making final arrangements for our meeting in Lisbon.

May 23: Took Miss (Annabelle) Johnson to the University and met with Dr. Stanford and Jack Parker for a recital of his trip and the various points of contact he had made with book sellers and others. We were sorry Dr. Morrill could not be present as he was out of the city. Dr. Stanford seems to be greatly pleased with Parker's presentation. He shows a good deal of ingenuity in his approaches and good judgment in his solutions. Discussed the matter of an assistant.

June 6: Reviewed with Stanford and Parker a list of acquisitions which have been offered as result of our recent trip. I am convinced we have picked up a lot of valuable material at reasonable prices. In some cases I doubt whether the dealer really knew what he had. Our advantage lies in the fact that we have a specific objective, in contrast to mere rarity of the item.

July 31: To the University after lunch. Saw Dr. Stanford and Mr. Parker. Reviewed new books which have been submitted. I am greatly pleased with the nature and scope of these acquisitions. Some of them are not only germane to our field but are rare in character.

October 23: In the evening dinner of the Friends of the Library. Interesting group with Professor (Francis M.) Rogers of Harvard the principal speaker. I think he took for granted that his audience was much more informed than it actually was, and stressed the religious aspects out of proportion to the small reference to trade.... The Minnesota Press is out with our new book "From Lisbon to Calicut", which is very beautifully done.

November 13: Attended a dinner of the specialized librarians at the Campus Club. A very interesting group, with enthusiastic acceptance of Parker's talk. Later a visit to the Bell Room at the library.

November 14: Parker is in this morning with some new items submitted to us. They seem for the most part to be desirable. We are short of cash on our 1956 budget but shall manage to handle it some way. Discussed with Parker the expansion of the catalog work which Miss Johnson has inaugurated. He has given us a very clear picture of the divisions of historical importance of our different fields and their classification into periods, which shows he has a very keen grasp of the problem.

1957 Diary.

April 2, 1957. Sailed for Europe on the S.S. UNITED STATES.

April 10: (Madrid) Spent the day running back and forth with Parker and Miss Enriqueta Gurrea-Nozaleda, the interpreter who is working for us. Seems to be a very intelligent girl. No one seems to keep appointments. Hard to make contacts.

April 17: (Madrid) With the book dealers in the morning. Lunched with the Byingtons. In the afternoon again with the book-dealers.

April 25: (Milan) Off at 8:30 to Milan. This is another holiday—Liberation Day. We called on Senora (Carla) Marzoli. She is quite a girl. She is certainly a human dynamo with a loud voice and a loud laugh, and she talks so fast and so much that one would be exhausted in a little while. She has a very nice shop. Our discussion centered around the portolan and we have decided we would pay the price. Reviewed Mrs. Marzoli's books. She has a few items; nothing of significance. As everybody else was closed we went out to the industrial fair but there was such a mass of people it was impossible to make headway against the crowd, much to our disappointment. We returned to the hotel.

April 29: (London) In London. Most of the day with the tailors, Trickers, and the book sellers. They do not seem to have very much. They say we have wiped the market out.

May 7: (Paris) With Parker visiting booksellers. Our first call was Santoni. This is rather an experience. A knock on the door brought Mrs. Santoni, revealing a very narrow hall stacked on each side with books. She had to back up toward the bedroom to let us in, and when we closed the door we had to back into Santoni's office, which I think was not over 8 x 10. Just a desk in the center, flanked with at least three or four tiers of books, all stacked on top of each other. Just space for a small desk and one chair. How in the world he knows what he has is beyond belief. They say the best things are under the bed in his room. I can well believe this, but how he and his wife get into bed is more than I can see because there too the room was stacked to the ceiling. He loves books, which are his life. He knows every item he has.

May 28: Jack Parker is back. We have reviewed some of the suggested purchases and these will go through when, as and if they are confirmed on examination. Dick Anderson says we have enough money to meet these oncoming bills, but we may want for some special reason to defer some until the early part of next year. The expense is running pretty high.... Entertained Dr. and Mrs. Stanford, Mr. and Mrs. John Parker, and Miss Johnson at dinner. A pleasant evening.

1958 Diary.

March 27: Spent the morning with Dr. Stanford and Jack Parker, who came out to the new building. Discussed the necessary expansion of the room into additional space to accommodate the users.

May 1: Long confidential talk with Dr. (President James L.) Morrill, first in respect to the future of the library and what assistance we might expect in the way of its perpetuation. It is evident that they have discussed the matter among themselves and are hopeful that I might now come to some conclusion about the terms of the will, to make an immediate gift. This I wish to give consideration to. I also talked with Dr. Morrill about the future status of the University, pointing out that the ambitions of the citizens of the State to compete with all the other states in having a great university should be tempered by the thought of whether we can afford it. Certainly we cannot expect to enjoy such incomes as are inherent in the industrial states. How much can we afford? I am still convinced we will have no full realization of our ability to afford this until such time as an investigation is made into the net balance of trade in the State and I am hopeful some research may be erected within the university to accomplish this purpose.... Had a talk with Dr. Stanford. I find from my talk with him that he reflects the same attitude as the President. They feel the university has tried to carry out its part of the program and the stipulations, and it would be gratifying if they would receive the assurance of possession of the library, which is not definite under the terms of my will. I have suggested that Dr. Morrill, Mr. Willey and Dr. Stanford meet with me and with the trustees and see what can be worked out. Of course I told him I might have an exaggerated idea of the importance of the library and we should have an independent appraisal. I want to know if the name attached to it is standing in the way of its support, and what we might expect in the way of future accommodations. He tells me, as does Dr. Morrill, that the present library facilities will pass into a research stage and that the student material will have to be transferred to new buildings with more ample facilities.... My talk with Dr. Stanford involved getting Mrs. Vera Bowman to take over the Friends of the Library and their ability to take some of the risks involved, as the latter is very dynamic and no doubt if she took on the job would be very alive and alert and might be advancing ideas of procedures which are not in keeping with their thinking. However, in my opinion this is a risk we must take.... Stanford said (Vsevolod "Steve") Slessarev (Assistant Curator) had been making inquiries as to his future. He told him he was young and he thought he should settle down and find out what it was all about before getting himself exercized; that he had assurance of the next year but he could not give him any assurances beyond that. It all depends upon how matters develop. He spoke in the highest terms of Mr. Parker. Said he considered his performance outstanding and he was a man who might be classified as irreplaceable.

June 9: I had a nice visit from Jack Parker this morning, who brought in a list of the books and manuscripts, briefly described, which he calls the "first priority" items resulting from his recent trip. These are to the value of a little over $31,000. I think he has chosen well and wisely. Many of the items have been secured at very favorable prices, much less than if we were dependent upon the local United States book dealers.... Later I had a visit from Dr. Morrill, Dean Willey and Dr. Stanford, whom I entertained at lunch and gave a brief tour of the building. They are concerned about the future of the library. They have expressed a very great appreciation of what it means. They would like some changes in the provisions of the will conveying it to them, so that they have assurance it will be here, which will permit them to justify the expense they have incurred and to encourage others to contribute—which would not be possible without some guarantee that the books would find permanent lodging. They are willing to have the Regents enter into a mandate guaranteeing me of the terms which I have prescribed regarding the permanency of support and the further development of the library. I shall take this up with the trustees.

July 17: Spent the morning at the library at the University going over the new acquisitions. Parker has done a superb job. He is going on to Philadelphia and will check on (John) Fleming to see if we can work out an exchange with books which Fleming had valued for us. If this can be done, it would certainly cut down the price at which the Pigafetta sold! Parker is going on to spend a week in Washington on the completion of his PhD thesis on which he has another year's work.

July 21: Had a talk with Dick Anderson about the letter from President Morrill in respect to the library. We are discussing some of the items which we will want to incorporate in any understanding with the University looking to the transfer of the title.

September 15: Conference with President Morrill, (Deans Malcolm Willey and William T. Middlebrook, Dr. Stanford, and Dick Anderson were also present). We discussed informally the future of the Bell library and have tried to formulate terms and conditions which would permit the transfer of title to the books to the University and their future care and development. The University group brought forth the idea that it would be easier for the University to administer costs and to have any income from an endowment or foundation flow into the university for purposes of travel and acquisition. I think this is a point well taken. There was an expression on the part of Middlebrook that endowment funds be paid into the hands of the university, but I should be very much opposed to it. The endowment funds should be in the hands of the book trustees and I am confident that the investments would receive better attention and would be productive of larger income than they would in the mill run of University investments. However, I have no objection to leaving a loophole for the trustees to divest themselves of this responsibility and transfer it to the University when and as it becomes evident that this would prove to be of greater advantage. I have asked them to set forth in very rough summary their own views and we will try to do the same and hold another meeting, at which time we hope we can formalize the proposals.

November 13: Jack Parker was in and I reviewed with him the agreement we have drawn up for consideration of the Board or Regents in respect to the library. I find Parker extremely keen, very much alive to the situation, and with some helpful suggestions.

1959 Diary.

March 25: I came home from Georgia on the ninth. Unfortunately that evening I had what is truly a slight stroke, which has resulted in nasal hemorrhages, which failing to respond to ordinary treatment required hospitalization from which I am apparently working my way back with entirely different physiological conditions. One must be realistic. Between the hospital and the hemorrhages I have been laid up most of the time since my return.

April 10: Long day at the Regents meeting. We are naturally in a state of alarm over the failure of the legislature to pass measures which would insure proper revenues for the university's budget. It looks as if curtailments were inevitable. This will result in an advance of tuition which will be rather wide-sweeping in effect upon students with limited means at their command.

May 20: Some time ago Dr. (John) Bowditch of the History Department at the university invited me to lunch, but I requested to be the host and to entertain some members of the department. Today at the Minneapolis Club I had luncheon with Messrs. Bowditch, (John B.) Wolf, (Burton)

Stein, (Paul W.) Bamford and (David Harris) Willson, together with Dean Blegen, Mr. Willey, Dr. Stanford and Mr. Parker. Dr. Bowditch expressed a great interest on the part of the history department in the collection and a desire on their part to enhance its usefulness with various suggestions to that end, including an advanced scholarship and the inclusion of microfilms of material that there is no possibility of acquiring by purchase. In reply to the various helpful suggestions that came from various members, I tried to make it clear that of course the ownership of the library now rests with the University, who have complete control over the use policies of the collection as is. Naturally all procedures for use would come from the library department in a normal way, but that they could rest assured that I had a very sympathetic and receptive attitude toward these suggestions and would be glad to shape my future contributions along lines which could be mutually agreed between them and the head of the library and Mr. Parker.... Later in the day Dean Willey called me up to express great appreciation for the meeting and the feeling that the meeting had been very constructive.... During the course of the luncheon I talked with him about the attack which had been made on the University about the appearance there of (Mikhail) Menshikov, which apparently greatly disturbed President Morrill. Naturally I am in great sympathy with Dr. Morrill's efforts to have an expression of opinion on the important subject of trade from those who are causing us the greatest concern. It seems to be that the segment of the public who demand freedom of expression is not extending that same freedom of expression to others. How shall we know what the thinking and attitude of Russia is and what their methods are unless we hear from them? And how can we be informed as to intelligent and constructive ways of meeting them unless we have occasion to hear directly from them their side of the story? The expression of criticism on the part of some of the Regents is unbelievable. Willey felt that a letter to Dr. Morrill would be very helpful, and I am very glad to respond.

June 2: Jack Parker was in and we have discussed some interesting items which I think will eventually prove to be valuable items, although at present they are modestly priced. He is planning to take a short vacation, after which he will go abroad, pressing into new territories in the hope that we can uncover desirable material.

August 16: I passed my eightieth birthday very quietly and happily, going down to Afton with Charlie and Lucy and little Lucy.

October 15: Jack Parker is back from Europe with his report of items on which he has obtained options. I think it is quite a remarkable performance. He has secured 13 items in the 15th century, 17 in the 16th, and 11 in the 17th and 2 in the 18th. These all sound very desirable. Of course final determination cannot be made until after they have been submitted to the usual course of examination.... Parker feels we are getting a relationship now with the dealers that is intimate and helpful. Knowing our desires they are all the more keen to obtain items and to see that they are offered to us. He gave me the report that Maggs have bent from their rigid attitude of offering nothing until the catalog is published and are now evidencing some pre-consideration to our interests.

1960 Diary.

April 27: Spent the afternoon with (H.P.) Kraus. He is taking a very firm position with regard to the prices he is advancing at a rate that I think is all out of proportion to the values. He is in a commanding position, and apparently with availability of credit that will permit him to go into book build-up prices as a protection to his own stock. He tells me he intends to attend both the Sotheby sale and the one in Geneva. I think under the circumstances we shall have to let him act as our agent, with the understanding that if the prices we authorize are exceeded and he secures the items, that we will still have an opportunity to re-purchase them on a ten percent commission basis, provided we act within a reasonable time after the sale. The man is not well, but he certainly is in the saddle so far as the book market is concerned.

August 16, 1960. This is my 81st birthday. I wonder that I have survived so long, but I am most grateful for all my blessings.

Edward B. Stanford

A Dream Come True

THE year was 1953. The month was October. Looking back after four decades it was a memorable time for the University of Minnesota libraries.

Quietly, for a good many years, James Ford Bell had been collecting books of note and antiquarian value but without any sharply defined topical focus. Among his holdings, for example, were works as diverse as original Shakespeare folios and a partial file of seventeenth century "Relations", reports from dedicated servants of the Society of Jesus in the New World back to their superiors in Europe.

It was in 1953 that Mr. Bell formulated his goals for the collection we now know as the James Ford Bell Library, and completed the magnificent room that was to provide a fitting home for it as a gift to the University. It was also in that year that, with the appointment of Dr. John Parker as Curator, the future for his collection, that Mr. Bell had so carefully envisioned, began coming to fruition, marked by that memorable October dedication.

The distinguished array of perceptive historical studies that have resulted from painstaking research in Bell Library resources since then bear eloquent witness to the viability of the significant role Mr. Bell envisioned for his collection so many years ago.

My own first recollection of Mr. Bell goes back to when, during my first year in charge of the University Libraries, he invited me to his downtown office to see some of the books he had been collecting over the years. At that time *Jesuit Relations* meant little to me, so what most impressed me among the treasures he showed me then were his several original Shakespeare folios, which any rare book collector would have given his right arm to own. I reacted with some degree of shock, therefore, when Mr. Bell later told me of his intention, ultimately to sell these renowned imprints. After all, most collectors, once having acquired them, would not even consider voluntarily giving up any genuine folios of Shakespeare!

By the time he was ready to take such bold action, Mr. Bell had had time to discuss with me the long-range focus he had developed for his collection, and his plan to dispose of items, however valued, that did not contribute to that end. In this context, selling off non-relevant books not only made good business sense, but also enhanced the scholarly integrity of the collection as a whole, as a resource for future research.

As I came to know Mr. Bell personally in time, I began to appreciate what a foresighted and discriminating collector he really was. He not only limited his purchases to items that contributed to the focused plan he had adopted for the collection. He also set high standards for the publications and maps he did buy. Among his criteria in evaluating items various dealers offered to him were the edition of such works, and, insofar as possible, their physical integrity and condition. Although he wanted to have represented in his holdings varied editions of specific works, which may reflect differences in translation, textual changes over time, and even additions and deletions from the original version in its first printing, he wanted the collection to have the author's own expression whenever it could, in the realization that such original texts, in the author's own words, best reflect the tenor of the time when the work was first written.

Condition, a characteristic of a book that sometimes is not considered important to collectors, especially when a noteworthy item is offered at a seemingly "bargain" price, was an important consideration for Mr. Bell. He often turned down items with missing prints or maps, properly believing that these features of a publication are usually significant for the comprehension and understanding of an author's text.

This reminiscence has emphasized the vision and prescience that motivated James Ford Bell to build such a dynamic research collection for the University of Minnesota. The Bell Library embodies the belief he held that it was primarily commerce and trade, whether in men's souls or in raw materials and goods, that was a catalyst for the intrepid adventurers and risk-takers who braved unknown waters and lands to test the potential of hitherto undeveloped territories for material or spiritual profit. And for this the University and the many scholars who have used the collection are in debt to Mr. Bell.

The observance of this notable anniversary of the events of 1953 should not pass, however, without mention of the role of Jack Parker, whose own vision and understanding of the relevance of the collection to the economic and political problems of our own day, did so much to make possible the fulfillment of Mr. Bell's goals. With the highest scholarly integrity Jack worked with some of the world's most knowledgeable antiquarian book dealers to add, item by item, elusive pieces of the record of European Expansion, for the use of future historians. He also had a knack for interpreting new acquisitions for scholars and laymen alike, in a way that made musty old manuscripts come to life with relevance for today's generation of students, politicians, and readers. Now that Dr. Parker has retired, this assessment can be expressed openly.

Together James Ford Bell and Jack Parker were two outstanding men of dedication, whose combined efforts to create a research resource have made a significant difference, not only to Minnesota but throughout the literate world.

The year 1953 was a memorable one for the University Library. This year of 1993 is also an appropriate time to look back on the Bell Library and remind ourselves of how a forty-year old vision has produced results that have more than lived up to the expectations of its author.

James Ford Bell

Bound Fragments of Time

I READ recently a brilliant article by Dr. Ralph Gerard of the University of Illinois College of Medicine in which he tosses off striking ideas at the rate of one to each line. His fundamental purpose is to define *memory*, but in the process of doing so he offers also a new suggestion about the essential character of a library. Examining his subject from the point of view of a nerve physiologist, but at the same time with the insight of a poet, Dr. Gerard presents this striking series of challenges:

> Do trees "remember" good and bad seasons in the thickness of their rings?
>
> Is a film a memory of light in chemicals, and a tape recording a memory of sound in magnetism?
>
> Is a library a memory of thoughts in books and a brain a memory of thoughts in protoplasm?

Yes, I think we may say that a book "remembers" the thoughts of the man who set it down. Perhaps it is permissible to complete Dr. Gerard's definition by saying that *a library is a memory of the experiences, actions, and achievements of man—in ink.*

What need is it, then, that makes a particular man wish to bring together a particular collection of those memories?

It is, I think, man's insatiable appetite for experience. He wishes to live not only his own life but the lives of many other men as well, especially the lives of men whose preoccupations are similar to his own.

With the many instinctual prohibitions imposed by an advancing culture comes the need for compensating interests. This is displayed in many ways. Gradually the diverting interests take shape, and often they express themselves in material form. One seeks those objects which reflect his interests. He awakens to the possessive urge to gather them about him. He treasures them for those qualities which bespeak his interest, often far better than his own words. They form the historical background of his present cultural environment.

He, in effect, becomes a collector.

No doubt the primitive arrow-maker, as he developed under the influence of his craft, noted with pride the improvements he was able to conceive and incorporate into his product, or to draw from the examples of other craftsmen that came to his observation in trade or as spoils of war. No doubt, in his simple way, he treasured the examples of these changes, not only because of any material beauty they may have possessed, but equally as symbols of his craft. He too, in his way, became a collector.

Call it a diversion of thought and interest if you will, but collecting is one of the factors leading away from primitive instincts to controlled civilization.

This characteristic of collecting takes many forms and reflects the diversity of man's thoughts and interests. The many facets it presents contribute to the entire culture in which we live and develop.

Our purpose at the moment is the consideration of one object of this collecting characteristic: the written and the printed word—an invaluable aid to man's memory of events past and present.

Here are recorded events and experiences—things that had happened or were happening—records that authenticated and gave substance to the acts they recorded, pictures and charts which helped reduce these tales to reality. All these were substantiated reports, free from the distortions of the sagas and legends that have come down to us from the past—barring always those imaginative impulses that may have colored the record!

Yet beneath even the most imaginative record there is usually an underlying activity of man to which we can point specifically—always with due regard, of course, for the authority from which the report originated.

I think it is only natural in each instance to ask oneself, "What is the underlying reason which prompted *this* collection?" For, consciously or unconsciously, a course is formulated and a collection takes a specific direction.

As I look back on the genesis of my own effort in collecting books and seek a reasonable explanation for it, I have a recurring thought that it concerns itself with *trade*. Being in trade, I was perhaps influenced, without knowing I was influenced, by this environment.

Trade, to me, is an expression of the world's economy of living. Each individual seeks to live, and to live advantageously. His needs may not be fully served by his own efforts, nor his desires satisfied with what is immediately available. If he has a surplus of things of his own production, he uses it as a medium to secure other things from those who have an available supply.

Thus, in the beginning only simple barter, trade swelled in volume, developed new techniques, and widened the field of its contacts.

Trade in itself is basically a selfish interest. Trade knows no border, no kin, no breed, no loyalty or patriotism or sentiment. Trade goes on regardless of wars, riots, and commotions. Trade seeks avenues of advantage even as between enemies. Always it searches for that which serves its interests best.

From the earliest days of man, once he had discovered the necessity and value of trade, his operations multiplied and expanded. As he journeyed afield, he met conflicting operations, for the advantages of trade developed first tribal interests and later nationalism as we know it today, where groups in self-protection of evidenced interests or desires seek trade preference or control, often at the expense of others.

Trade preyed upon other trade, and in turn was preyed upon. In a desire to avoid these conflicting interests came a search for other routes, other means of obtaining trade ends, under more favorable conditions. This in turn led to journeys and explorations in the development of new lands, or the exploitation of new fields and new peoples. Always the search has been for an easier and a better way.

As this trading instinct led man farther and farther afield, he came to the barriers of the East with its controlled and expensive trade routes, with its wealth of gold, of fine raiment, and of spices. Man overcame his fear of the sea and sought water routes to these riches, as shorter and safer than overland travel.

Gradually he pierced the unknown, and having acquired the knowledge that the world is round, his imagination conceived that he might meet the East by going West!

And so, in his search for shorter routes, he came upon this continent of ours, mistakenly believing it to be the outskirts of Cathay. But, his mistake discovered, he still pursued his search for the route to Cathay, trying by way of the South, by way of the Northwest, and even by way of the Northeast. And, in all these journeyings to which trade drove him on, he discovered that even in these primitive, unknown lands trade routes and trade controls already existed!

It was natural that after such journeyings a man should seek to set down reminders of what he had experienced, of his observations, his discoveries, his adventures. At first these were but manuscripts, the work of his own hands or the copyings of scribes; but, with the invention of printing, the dissemination of his memoirs could be greatly broadened and his vanity sought to have the voice of his exploits more widely heard.

It may be said that the tomes which embody a man's works or observations are merely printed words, and that these can be reproduced, or presented more clearly and with better technique, by later writers and in later editions. But even the most advanced methods of reproduction cannot truly embody the quality—expressively intimate and personal—of an ORIGINAL EDITION, for this presents the authentic environment of the author and the spirit of his times in a way that is wholly lacking in later reproductions. One takes the FIRST EDITION from the very hands that touched and formed it. A reprint, therefore, is merely a *reflection* of the thing, not the thing itself.

In my own collection of gleanings from the wealth of the past, I have tried to gather together the basic records of trade and subsequent exploration which led to the discovery of this country. It is my hope that the collection will be expanded along the lines that depict the progress of trade as it touched upon the shores of this country and found herein already-established trade routes which led man on to traverse the width and breadth of this continent and contributed to its development and continuing success.

In conclusion a word about my satisfaction in turning my collection over to the University of Minnesota. It is my hope that these books may make a contribution to the task of fulfilling the nature of man which every educational institution is designed to perform. I derive my feeling about the nature of man from a fine statement once made by the late Alfred Korzybski, creator of the Institute of General Semantics. Korzybski spoke of the remarkable capacity which is peculiar to man. He said:

> I mean the capacity to summarize, digest and appropriate the labors and experiences of the past;
>
> I mean the capacity to use the fruits of past labors and experiences as intellectual capital for the developments in the present;
>
> I mean the capacity to employ as instruments of increasing power the accumulated achievements of all precious lives of past generations spent in trial and error, trial and success;
>
> I mean the capacity of human beings to conduct their lives in the ever increasing light of inherited wisdom;
>
> I mean the capacity in virtue of which man is at once the inheritor of by-gone ages and the trustee of posterity.
>
> And because humanity is just this magnificent natural agency by which the past lives in the present and the present in the future, I define humanity, in the universal tongue of mathematics and mechanics, to be *the time-binding class of life*.

So, then, to reading, thinking members of the noble time-binding class, I am happy to offer for their use certain fragments of time bound up in books.

This collection does not loom large alongside other great libraries. And yet, everything must have a beginning, and the great libraries throughout the world were once small both in extent and purpose. What I have collected has been carefully chosen and is, I think, of a quality and an extent to form at least the nucleus of a library which—with the interest and help of the university and the local community—may someday take its place with the others both in its extent and in the values it offers. I sincerely hope that it may help to make the generations of students that will pass through the University of Minnesota good trustees for posterity of the boldness, confidence, vision, and wisdom which these books contain as gifts from the past.

(This was the talk Mr. Bell gave on October 30, 1953, at the dedication of his Library at the University of Minnesota.)

John Parker

Remembering the Early Years

JAMES Ford Bell's most memorable words at our first meeting were "I would like someone to manage the Library whose mind has not been made up about too many things." That prescription for a curator was a reflection of the mind of the builder who was not at all sure what the building would be. There was as he noted in his essay "Bound Fragments of Time" a collection "carefully chosen ... of a quality and an extent to form at least the nucleus of a library" but he saw it as a nucleus only, a beginning whose growth and direction were not predetermined by the nucleus alone but would be determined by the energies and ideas brought to it. One characteristic of this Library was firmly imbedded in the nucleus, and this is reflected in his essay in which he wrote "I define humanity in the universal tongue of mathematics and mechanics, to be *the time-binding class of life,*" for this quality of humanity to him is what books were about, "the quality—expressly intimate and personal—of an ORIGINAL EDITION, for this presents the authentic environment of the author and the spirit of his times." That statement left no doubt that whatever the range of time or place or subject which the Library might eventually embrace, it would be a library authenticating its texts in first and other important early editions, and manuscripts wherever possible.

There were immediate goals in the early days of the Library despite unsettled boundaries for the scope of its collection. If our mind was not made up about too many things there were nevertheless established desiderata within the range of the nucleus which needed to be hunted down. While hunting these we could be exploring those realms in which we were less certain of direction. One of these desiderata was the famous Martin Waldseemüller Globe Gores of 1507, at that time the only copy known and the property of the Prince of Liechtenstein. It had been offered at auction in 1950, but bidding had not reached the reserve price placed on it. Would a private purchase be possible, and soon, before some other collector bought it? The Liechtenstein agent, Richard Zinser, was located and he brought the Globe Gores to Minneapolis in May, 1954, in a memorable plain brown paper wrapper. There was never a moment's doubt about the purchase. The gores, meant to be mounted on a sphere, carried the name America on that still-vague land mass in the western Atlantic and were a natural cornerstone for a Library whose image was still entirely associated with Americana.

Mr. Zinser made another visit, with another map. It was a brilliant manuscript depicting the 1725-29 route of Captain Vitus Bering across Siberia and then by sea past the promontory of Asia that faces Alaska. Was this Americana? Well, almost. And were we thinking about Americana only? Was our mind made up so soon? It was 1954 and we were facing the fact, as collectors, what we knew well as students of history, that America was not a primary end for Europe's earliest explorers and merchants. It was variously an obstacle or a hoped-for way station on the route to Asia. Could one sensibly collect only Americana if the Library's focus was to be on European commercial expansion? The Bering map was acquired, possibly as much on aesthetic as historic grounds.

It was most fortunate for our thinking about the Library's future that Harvard University Press published in 1952 a book by Boies Penrose titled *Travel and Discovery in the Renaissance*. Here was a study of the background of the Age of Discovery, and more than a century of post-Columbian voyages and travels to the eastern as well as the western hemisphere. Mr. Penrose, like James Ford Bell, was a knowledgeable collector, but with a primary interest in the East, and his book contained an excellent essay on the primary sources for the years his book covered. Mr. Bell's copy of that book made many a trip with him, as business concerns took him to New York regularly, and the pages came to have innumerable underlinings, question marks in the margins, queries about the sources Mr. Penrose cited. Very early in its history, Mr. Penrose became a great friend and source of information for the development and direction the Library would eventually assume.

Another book which heightened Mr. Bell's interest in the East was Henry H. Hart's *Sea Road to the Indies*, a chronicle of early Portuguese voyages to India. Such books spoke to his passion to seek beginnings in all things: historical movements, mechanical inventions, business procedures, manufacturing processes. He would ask intuitively, what was it that prompted or preceded what is generally accepted as the beginning? As a collector of Americana he could not begin the history of the New World with Columbus. What was it that moved Columbus to his enterprise—what intellectual environment, what commercial pressures? In all of this thinking the Portuguese navigators of the fifteenth century came to the fore as the immediate predecessors, and before them the merchants, the pilgrims, the adventurers who brought the Middle Ages to a larger world view than Europe had enjoyed since the Roman Empire. And there were the scholars too, reaching back to antiquity for the most plausible theories and descriptions of the earth's geography that were to be found, to be broadcast anew by Johann Gutenberg's new invention. The approach to beginnings of Europe's Age of Discovery seemed possible, if vast.

There were other types of beginnings to be investigated. What was the nature of European—and world—commerce before the Age of Discovery, and where were the records of it? Such questions took our thinking to European archives, to collections of Mesopotamian clay tablets in Europe, in North America, and in the Near East. What were the possibilities for collecting? And what was the commerce of North and South America before the Europeans disrupted it? What were the routes over which it moved? What goods followed those routes? Here we were looking over the edge of Western culture into a world where records were less available than in ancient Mesopotamia and were largely in the form of artifacts, the preserve of museums and anthropologists.

And there were beginnings within the memory of our time. Who was keeping the records of the twentieth century revolution in transportation and trade, the plotting and development of air traffic routes and networks which overcame both land and sea barriers to continue what the generation of Columbus had begun? Could the technology of microphotography reduce these records to a size to be managed in a library? Many of the pioneers of this latter age of discovery were still with us. Would they be interested in helping?

While thinking about these things, exploring them, and gradually rejecting them in the late 1950s because they were simply too vast to be managed within one library, the work that was possible went forward. Back to the desiderata list. The prime desideratum was Pierre Biard's *Relation de la Nouvelle France*, Lyon, 1616. This was the first account of a Jesuit mission in Canada, the foundation stone for any collection of French Americana, and especially for a collection of *Jesuit Relations of New France*, an area in which the James Ford Bell Collection was internationally renowned. But it did not have the Biard volume. Mr. Bell had passed up an opportunity to acquire it in the early 1950s, being of the impression that there were two copies available to him when in fact there appeared in retrospect to have been one copy offered by two booksellers, and it went to another collector. So wherever Americana was bought and sold Mr. Bell held out hope that another copy of Father Biard's book would show up. Eventually it did—after seventeen years.

And so probing the universe of time and space, seeking to outline a scope for this Library while scouring the shelves of booksellers in North America and Europe for items that fit into the collection as it existed, new directions emerged, always with the principle in mind that new directions would be built upon the strengths of the "original collection." That strength, of course, was North Americana, the result of Mr. Bell's desire to get at the origins of European commerce in this continent, and most specifically the heartland of the continent here in Minnesota. But just as Minnesota's European connection started with Jacques Cartier and the anonymous fishermen who preceded him, it was obvious that the objective of the early penetrations of these northern waterways by Cartier, Champlain, Hudson and others the objective was always a route to Asia, and if commerce was the goal, then what was the nature of the commerce that was hoped for? The Portuguese were describing it in their early narratives of voyages to India. The pressure to find a western route was clearly the result of the success of the eastern route around the Cape of Good Hope. So what books described this eastern enterprise? Penrose's *Travel and Discovery in the Renaissance* gave a fair sampling. There were booksellers indeed who specialized in the literature of Portuguese history and overseas expansion, some of them in

Portugal, some in England, some scattered about the bookselling community. And nearly every bookseller has a category of books called "Voyages and travels." Here lay ample opportunity to build a library with the assistance of those whose livelihood was supplying books and manuscripts. One of these was Dr. Maurice Ettinghausen who presided over the rare books at the firm of A. Rosenthal in Oxford with an enthusiasm for Portuguese books that bordered on fanaticism. He had been librarian to the last Portuguese king, Manuel II in the early 1920s and had produced a great three volume catalog of King Manuel's library. Subsequently he had catalogued Spanish and Portuguese books for Maggs Bros. of London, known world wide for its stock of voyage and travel literature, including great catalogs of Spanish and Portuguese books. In the early 1950s the book world was chasing Americana far more actively then books about Asia, so the James Ford Bell Library became the dominant prospect for early accounts of Portuguese voyages to Asia. Dr. Ettinghausen provided cornerstones for our new direction with the great multi-volume chronicles of João de Barros, Fernão Lopes de Castanheda, and Diogo do Couto in their first editions. These acquisitions came in 1955 and with them on the shelves there was a feeling that the Library was looking beyond what it had been to what it might become.

Throughout Europe booksellers quickly learned of this "new" library and its emphasis, for it is fair to say that in a life crowded with business concerns Mr. Bell had relied primarily on a few booksellers in New York and London, primarily H.P. Kraus, Henry Stevens, Son & Stiles, and Lathrop C. Harper. Between the sixteenth and eighteenth century every country in Western Europe had in some degree developed an Eastern commerce, usually through an East India company, and all of these contacts had generated a literature describing the East and its commercial and other opportunities. All had published numerous regulations upon the administration of that trade. If the New World had been a new world to Renaissance Europe, the Old World of Africa and Asia became the new world of the James Ford Bell Library.

The materials available for acquisition were not significantly different from those pertaining to the Americas: newsletters, geographies, travel narratives, missionary reports, conquest literature, regulatory laws and decrees. But there was difference in content. Europeans in Asia were encountering a highly sophisticated commercial network developed over centuries: merchants from Japan trading in Indonesia, Chinese merchants and goods everywhere, spices and cloth moving back and forth between islands and mainland. Specialty products identified with one town or island moving among the others. The Americas in the early years offered little of this, and Mr. Bell was not enthusiastic about conquistador narratives. Trade was what he wanted to emphasize in his collecting, and the East fit that interest admirably. Indeed he was like a merchant discovering a new market: new booksellers, new subjects, a new geography of routes and markets. The commitment made, the book trade must be combed for booksellers and materials. And all the while, of course, the old emphasis on Americana was not in the least to be neglected.

That Americana collection was renowned particularly for its *Jesuit Relations of New France*, an annual series of small books extending from 1632 to 1672. Their place in a library with a commercial emphasis was justified by their reportage of France's westward expansion through the St. Lawrence-Great Lakes waterway system, and the steady growth of the fur trade along that route. This was a manageable literature, collected by several great libraries, well described in library catalogues. Mr. Bell knew it intimately, the names of the editors—Le Jeune, Lalemant, Brissani, etc., the bibliographic points between editions and issues, the contents of each volume. The new Eastern emphasis, and his passion to get as near as possible to the beginnings of things confronted Mr. Bell with the reality that the New France Jesuits were really the third generation of the Society of Jesus. Jesuits had been in India for more than seventy years before they seriously undertook Canada, and they had been in China and Japan for half a century. Canada was indeed a very small part of this world-wide missionary effort, and the literature of the other missions dwarfed the *Relations* from Canada. What to do about this? Open the door to all of them. Thus began the assembling of missionary reports—not only Jesuit reports—on Portuguese progress in India, religious and commercial, of priests and merchants in the Spice Islands, of Father Matteo Ricci and his successors in China, of the Spanish presence in the Philippines, of conflict and power politics in Ethiopia, of footholds in Vietnam. And it is not uncommon in the collected reports of missionaries to have Macao, Angola, and Brazil on adjacent pages, all Portuguese colonies, documentation of the realities of empire and the realities of collecting the literature of the empire. For the empire builder and the collector it was one world, and the record of it in books was no more divisible than was its trade.

For the collector of books nothing is more natural than moving out from an area of intense interest to an adjacent field, from the well-known to the somewhat known, the territory just outside the "borders" of the collection. But here was a leap beyond the familiar geography of North America into much less known territory, away from familiar waterways and beaver haunts into the crowded marketplaces of India and China. The gap could be bridged because of the type of book, the reports of Jesuit missionaries which retained strong elements of similarity regardless of the point of origin. But of course the contents would be new and different. Pierre Biard in Nova Scotia was concerned largely with mere survival and with making some beginnings for the faith among Indian children; Matteo Ricci in China was determined to make his way among the mandarins by engaging them in deep philosophical discussions in their own language.

But if this was to be a library with a truly world-wide scope, then it must encompass reportings of every aspect of the European presence abroad. Always seeking the beginnings of things, James Ford Bell warmed to these books of churchmen who defined the cultures of Africa and Asia for

Europeans, inviting their interest in further commitment, increased investment to begin the age of modern world commerce which he so ardently sought to document. If the names of Francis Xavier, Matteo Ricci, Alessandro Valignani, Luis Froes and others among eastern missionaries never became as familiar as their North American counterparts in James Ford Bell's lifetime, their importance to the Library's future was accepted with enthusiasm.

The books, maps, and manuscripts we sought were not merely mundane reports. They were often chronicles of important and exciting events, and sometimes with strong aesthetic appeal as well. "Bound Fragments of Time" were a wide-ranging assortment of materials. The early acquisition of the Bering map already mentioned was an interesting introduction to the possibilities. A German newsletter of 1505 titled in translation *The Way from Lisbon to Calicut, Mile by Mile* with its crude little woodcut map, the earliest printed map to trace that important route by sea to India, was at the other end of the aesthetic spectrum but was not less exciting for its primitiveness and its presumed utility as a document of public awareness of and speculation about the newly opened route to the East. And nearly a century later a very private document, a manuscript letter from the Dutch captain Olivier van Noort told of his seeking a passage by the other southern route, the Strait of Magellan, as a useful outlet for the emerging Dutch trade to the East Indies. Perhaps Mr. Bell's favorite acquisition among the Eastern items was the *Roteiro* of João de Castro, Portuguese commander of a fleet that in 1541 followed a Turkish flotilla into the Red Sea, all the way from Aden to Suez, mapping in exquisite full-and double page charts the harbors and other coastal features along the way, while commenting on navigational aspects en route in a fine manuscript hand. That this is the only complete contemporary exemplar of this *Roteiro* enhanced its attractiveness in his eyes. The fact that this *Roteiro* and the Van Noort letter came out of a London bookseller's vault on the same day—a bookseller previously unknown to him—opened up hopes that the aggressive seeker could find wonderful materials in this field of collecting, as yet so little exploited by collectors. Gone was the old system of relying upon a handful of booksellers to provide books and manuscripts in a collecting area well-known and understood as to what were the choicest items. Here was a world as a scope for collecting, and apart from some guidance from Penrose's book, no clear idea of what might become available, and every bookseller everywhere a possible source.

No place was written off as a possible hunting-ground in the 1950s: Cairo, Istanbul, Dubrovnik, Jerusalem, Warsaw were attempted. From Helsinki to Rome, and from Dublin to Berlin the search for books and booksellers went on, while of course the more familiar haunts, London, Paris, New York remained steady suppliers, but even in these much-traveled places there were booksellers we had not known, and who had not heard of the James Ford Bell Library. So collecting the early history of world trade became itself a world-wide enterprise. And of course the books came in, books often unknown to us until they were offered for sale. Not only books; maps as well.

The king of the hill in the London book trade in the 1950s was William H. Robinson Ltd., holders of vast quantities of high quality materials gathered between World Wars I and II, and managed with great skill by Lionel and Philip Robinson. No booksellers anywhere had better antennae for sensing what was happening in any part of the rare book world, and when the James Ford Bell Library became a reality at the University of Minnesota they were ready with an offering that would make a very big splash indeed. From their acquisition of the famous manuscript collection of Sir Thomas Phillips they had selected a Nautical Chart of 1424 for special analysis by Professor Armando Cortesão, the world's foremost authority on Renaissance cartography. Early in 1954 his monograph on the Chart was published by the University of Coimbra, surely with some help from the Robinsons. This Chart was the earliest known to show land far out in the western Atlantic. Was it real land, this blotch of red labeled Antillia, or was it one of the islands that time and imagination and legend had placed there? Or did it matter? It was an expression of belief in land far beyond any recorded voyage in 1424. The Robinsons sent us a copy of the book as soon as it was off the press with an option to buy the map. The Waldseemüller globe Gores had just been purchased. Robinson's offer was accepted, so within the space of four weeks Mr. Bell had acquired the two most important maps to come into the market to that date in the twentieth century. It was like two grand slam home runs in the first inning. And it was not just for the sake of making a splash in the market. These purchases represented a commitment by Mr. Bell to put great cornerstones under a library that would also include a lot of high quality if less spectacular items. It was above all a statement that quality is what this Library would be about.

In the early months of this Library's life the final section of a famous library was sold at Sotheby's in London. The Robert Hoe collection of Americana had been largely dispersed. The final catalog contained entries from the end of the alphabet. The W section was full of West Indische Compagnie materials, mostly pamphlets. Dutch Americana had enjoyed some popularity among American collectors, especially items pertaining to New Amsterdam. But the Dutch West India Company was important for the Dutch presence in Brazil, a strong presence in the first half of the seventeenth century, and for Dutch presence in the New World generally. Acquisition of several of the Hoe West India Company pamphlets set the Library on a course of gathering Dutch materials on their overseas enterprises which eventually established the Library as the dominant collection of this type of material in North America, and brought it into close relationship with the Dutch bookselling community, a very productive group including Nico Israel, Martinus Nijhoff, Maier Elte, B.M. Israel, Menno Hertzberger, among others.

The determination to bring the Far East into our collecting purview meant an opening to Dutch materials which told more about European trade in the East Indies than did books in any other language. And if Dutch West India Company pamphlets in their crowded black letter type were often not things of beauty, some volumes of the voyage literature were outstanding in their illustrative qualities. We discovered the "Golden Century" a period from about 1570 to 1670 during which Dutch art reached its highest quality—the time of Rembrandt after all—and a time when the Dutch were equally outstanding in shipbuilding, banking, navigation, cartography and publishing. So when the account of the first Dutch East India voyage, captained by Cornelis Houtman and reported by Willem Lodewicksz in 1598 was acquired in 1954 it became clear that for a modest cost the Library could add a volume with a fine map and many exquisite engravings giving it a strong aesthetic appeal and still maintain its primary emphasis on important texts. The Lodewicksz volume became a prototype for many subsequent additions of Dutch voyage literature.

But it was texts which were to be most important despite the Library's early notoriety for acquiring famous maps, and the easy temptation to show off illustrated works in the early exhibits that were mounted in the halls of Walter Library. Books like Lewes Roberts' *The Treasure of Traffic* (1641) excited James Ford Bell. With little visual appeal, apart from a single map, the book cataloged the merchandising that went on in many parts of the world, evidence of the developing world-wide commercial network of our time. Richard Jobson's *The Golden Trade* (1623) told of trade from the West African coast into the interior, not a pretty story by any means as it dealt in gold, ivory, and human beings with complete impartiality, but to Mr. Bell it was a part of the total picture of the commercial life of Africa, a commercial life that had existed before the Europeans arrived.

This pre-European era was a driving force in his collecting interests. The ways in which Europeans came to dominate existing trade networks, and to create new ones were important, of course, but beyond that—before that—there was trade, "an expression of the world's economy of living," with each individual a participant, disposing of a created surplus in exchange for what is in short supply. This fundamental human drive, almost an instinct, he sought in both primitive and in sophisticated societies. He wanted to document its existence and its importance in every way possible: to learn from the earliest European reports the routes that aboriginal trade followed, the goods that traveled those routes, the means of carrying the goods, the business practices that prevailed. All of these may have changed with the arrival and eventual dominance of Europeans, but the original impulse to trade surplus goods for needed goods was in his judgement the most exciting aspect of the history of commerce. He was in this regard more anthropologist than historian.

Yet he could get equally excited about the purely intellectual aspects of the early Age of Discovery. If knowledge of the earth, its lands, oceans, rivers, was fundamental to the concept of expanding a market or seeking new sources of supply, it was also fascinating to him as pure science. What did the earth mean to philosophers of earlier times, and how did maritime technology push at the borders of the known world? This too was a part of his endless effort to get to the beginnings of things. He delighted in early editions of Ptolemy's *Geographia*. In terms of tracing Renaissance discoveries against classical geography no book was more important, with its twenty-nine original maps reflecting the knowledge of the second century A.D., steadily augmented with maps showing the new discoveries. The handsome 1482 Ulm edition with its woodcut maps and the 1507 edition containing the famous Ruysch map of the world were the cornerstones of the Library's Ptolemy collection, neatly bracketing the voyages of Columbus and the earliest Portuguese voyages to India. Both of these volumes were in the Library before it came to the University, and they were the beginning of what has become a collection of twenty-five editions of that famous work, twelve of them added before Mr. Bell's death in 1961.

And Ptolemy was not the only classical authority of interest. Strabo, who lived in the first century A.D., was much more informative with respect to the economic and social life of the regions he described. Also, Strabo's *Geographia* was published earlier, in 1469. A major acquisition of 1956 was the second edition of Venice, 1472, still one of the most handsome typographic specimens in the Library. There would be several other early editions of Strabo's *Geographia*, but nothing to equal in importance or visual impact the earliest known Latin manuscript of the entire text, the first translation from Greek made by Guarino of Verona by commission of Pope Nicholas V, 1447-1455, a great patron of arts and learning. Here was something as close to the beginning of Western Europe's understanding of classical geography as it was possible to see. Two contemporary manuscripts of Guarino's translation are known, but this one alone contains the full-page portrait of Guarino in his ninetieth year, a portrait attributed to the school of Andrea Mantegna. In addition to the portrait the manuscript is richly endowed with ornamental initial letters. Once again, Mr. Bell was making a statement about the quality he intended to incorporate into this Library. Other classical geographies followed in distinctive editions: the remarkably beautiful Aldine first edition of Herodotus in Greek, 1503; early editions of geographies of Dionysius Periegetes, 1478; Pomponius Mela, 1482; Solinus, 1474-75; Macrobius, 1485; along with early editions of Pliny's *Historia Naturalis*, the *Bibliotheca Historica* by Diodorus Siculus, and the *Commentarii Greciam Describentes* by Pausanias. These were books that informed the Age of Discovery at its inception, and they continued to be published through much of the sixteenth century, sometimes with modifications to show the accrual of new knowledge, sometimes not, but in either case valuable as indicators of the high regard in which the classical geographers were held in the Renaissance.

In collecting the geographical background to the Age of Discovery we could not leap from the classics to the Renaissance humanists without regard to the medieval period, so attention was given to such works as Isidore of Seville's *Etymologiae*, a seventh century work first published in 1472, which includes the first world map ever printed in a book, the elementary T-O map dividing the circle of the world into three continents. More significant to the Age of Discovery was Pierre d'Ailly's *Imago Mundi*, a fourteenth-century geography which came into print in 1483 and is known to have been read by Columbus prior to his 1492 voyage. This was a "pre-Ptolemaic" geography in that Ptolemy's work was not generally available in Europe until after 1400, so Pierre d'Ailly's book has a unique niche in that it is a comprehensive world geography based on late medieval thought.

The emphasis given to geographical scholarship was not allowed to obscure the geographical insights gained by medieval and early Renaissance travelers which probably had a much larger impact on the ordinary reader. One of the prize possessions in the original Bell Collection was the first edition of Marco Polo's *Travels*, published in Nuremberg, 1477. A German edition, it is still one of only two known copies in the United States. Mr. Bell's interest in Marco Polo, surely one of the most famous merchants of all time, led him to acquire also the first Latin edition of Gouda, ca. 1483, and the first English edition of 1578. That beginning represented a commitment to acquire as many significant early editions of Marco Polo as possible, and soon the first French, Italian, and Spanish editions were added to the Library. Similarly the *Travels* of Sir John Mandeville, a fourteenth century writer, became important to the Library for this work, compiled from the writings of many travelers to the East, far outstripped Marco Polo's book in popularity. Some thirty-five editions of it were published between 1470 and 1500, most of which have been extremely rare for years. A great coup was the purchase of the first illustrated edition, Augsburg, 1481 containing a charming set of woodcuts portraying the fantasies in Mandeville's text. Yet that text contained some solid geographical thought also, which is generally overlooked.

As the explorers of Columbus's generation expanded Europe's geographical horizons and commercial possibilities it became increasingly apparent that their accomplishments were dependent upon the knowledge they brought to their tasks, and so the "background" element in the Library became increasingly important. One such work was Joannes de Sacro Bosco's *Sphaera Mundi*, a 13th century English mathematician's interpretation of the universe which had immense popularity in European universities after its first publication in 1472, and the source of several commentaries by later scholars who brought to it the more advanced cosmographical learning of the Renaissance. Some decisions had to be made in this area of astronomical, mathematical, and theoretic background to the navigation of the Age of Discovery. It became apparent that the books in those fields were numerous and could blunt the Library's progress in its primary mission which was to focus on the expansion of European overseas commerce. It was decided that books of this sort should be primarily of use in practical navigation more than theoretic or philosophical in tone. The dominant book of this type in the sixteenth century was the *Cosmographia* of Petrus Apianus, first published in 1524 and in many subsequent editions through the remainder of the sixteenth century. We acquired that first edition in 1958, and proceeded to add many others which represented changing interpretations by subsequent editors.

It was indeed the progression of editions of such books that came to give the emerging collection its sense of authority. In his "Bound Fragments of Time" Mr. Bell had extolled the first edition of an important work as paramount to the collector, and first editions never lost their place of priority for this Library. But in a collection that was attempting to track a historical development over four centuries, and that development was the discovery of the earth and its resources, then revision of knowledge was to be the essence of the subject matter. The very place of the earth in the universe incurred revision while Sacro Bosco and Apianus were popular, for Copernicus intervened and could not be ignored.

Books of navigation instruction presented similar opportunities for the Library to gather steadily increasing knowledge which was essential to the successful prosecution of long sea voyages. In his Original Collection was a great gem among navigation books, Pedro de Medina's *Arte de Navegar*, Valladolid, 1545. Yet when Mr. Bell acquired it he was not really interested in books on navigation. It was a map in the book which sold him on it, a woodcut chart of the Atlantic Ocean showing a rudimentary waterway reaching into the land mass of North America—the earliest representation of the St. Lawrence River, a reflection of Cartier's voyages, a Spanish adjunct to the very beginnings of his French Americana collection! But seeking a broader geographical scope meant that Medina's book, the first published book on oceanic navigation, was a keystone to the basic technology of trans-oceanic trade: possibly as important a book as we could imagine. So there were more editions of Medina's book to be acquired, and shortly William Bourne's *Regiment for the Sea*, 1596, the first comprehensive English book on the subject. In these years Mr. Bell's friend Henry Taylor was assembling a magnificent library on navigation to be presented to Yale University, and the Bell Collection made no attempt to rival it, but as a support to our interest in oceanic trade the Library needed some feeling for the tools of that trade. It was a pleasure one day in 1956 to have Mr. Taylor visit the James Ford Bell Library and to show him our few books on navigation, part of the "nucleus of a library" which he graciously admired.

Navigation, cosmography, geography, exploration, French Americana, trade—what was this Library about? An explanation was required by every undergraduate who came through the door of the beautiful room which announced that this must be a special place. Faculty members, library colleagues, university administrators, booksellers, needed to know too. For the first few years the explanation had to be in terms of goals which were gradually becoming clear, and roads to those goals which were not clear at all. We were merely on the way. But by the late 1950s (with 3,499 volumes by the end of 1959) we could say that this was a library about the origins and development of international trade from a European perspective, covering the period 1400 to 1800. The very vastness of the subject often bewildered the questioner. But there was an important question which we had to ask of the book world: what are the books that contained Europe's thoughts and theories about this expansion while it was going on? Were there policy debates, philosophical arguments, questions and justifications for all of this empire-building? Were there economists and philosophers who in their way were the equivalents of Ptolemy, Marco Polo or Medina?

It was not an easy question. The very pervasiveness of trade in all times and places which Mr. Bell had noted in his essay defined it as such an everyday subject in the lives of all people that it did not elicit great philosophical tomes on a frequent basis. The records of trade, alas, tend to get swallowed up in archives, or destroyed when a company fails, and here we were thinking about great national enterprises—East India companies, New World colonies, trading enterprises in Africa—what thinking led to their creation? How were they to be managed to the benefit of the nations that chartered and encouraged them?

There was no guide as convenient as Boies Penrose's book. The milestones in political economy were not as visible as Columbus or Magellan or Captain John Smith. But somehow in his earlier collecting Mr. Bell had acquired a first edition of Adam Smith's *Inquiry into the Nature and Causes of the Wealth of Nations*, 1776, a milestone in economics if ever there was one, but a late milestone. Who were the Adam Smiths of the sixteenth and seventeenth centuries who philosophized over the beginnings of the Age of Expansion? And how had trade been regulated and encouraged before the generation of Columbus? While we pondered the questions the answers began to show up in booksellers' catalogs—booksellers who at the beginning had no idea we were looking for such books. In 1954 we found John Evelyn's *Navigation and Commerce, Their Original and Progress*, 1674; Thomas Mun's great work on mercantilistic theory, *England's Treasure by Forraign Trade*, 1664; Francis Brewster's *Essay on Trade and Navigation*, 1695. The next year came Sir Dudley Digges' *The Defense of Trade*, 1615, and Andrew Yarranton's *England's Improvement by Sea and Land*, 1677. We were getting the feel of the discourse in political economy that went with overseas trade. We discovered that the national debates were about policy, and policy found expression in laws, hundreds of them. Often these were insignificant-looking leaflets of a few pages, but here were the laws chartering important companies, regulations upon specific imports and exports, notifications that the government had observed violations of one sort or another and would henceforth more vigorously prosecute smugglers, pirates, falsifiers of records, and a variety of other malefactors. These leaflets—English, French, Spanish, Portuguese, Dutch, Swedish were available in abundance at very low prices so the Library aggressively built up substantial holdings of these nuts and bolts of the European commercial experience abroad. This after all was what the great voyages and the great trading companies were about.

There was an aspect of law and regulation outside of these national expressions that called for attention also. Clearly the Age of European Expansion was an international scramble for wealth, a larger version of the competition among individuals and cities that had existed in earlier times. How was this earlier commerce managed so as to maintain some order among the competitors? What precedents were there to draw upon? The question pointed toward the history of maritime law, and commercial law of the Middle Ages, a formidable wilderness for book collectors. Good fortune in 1957 led to an offer of a 1519 edition of the *Consolat de Mar*, a collection of decisions by a maritime court in Barcelona going back to the eighth century, and steadily accruing both decisions and general acceptance by the mercantile community of the Mediterranean and Atlantic coastal areas so that it had almost the status of a code of international maritime law. The many editions of this work, beginning in 1484 testified to its usefulness and its authority, and it became for the James Ford Bell Library the beginning point for a modest collection of books on international custom and law in the management of overseas affairs. Under this umbrella of order came *De Iusto Imperio Lusitanorum*, 1625, by a Portuguese legal scholar Sepharino de Freitas in defense of Portuguese maritime presence in the East Indies; John Selden's *Mare Clausum*, 1636, and both were in response to Hugo Grotius's *Mare Liberum*, 1609, which was soon acquired along with his more famous *De Jure Belli ac Pacis*, 1625. In all of this thinking about laws governing trade, both theoretical and specific, the urge to find beginnings remained strong. How was the trade of Italy's great trading cities—Genoa, Venice, Florence—governed? The answer seemed to be in the laws and histories of those cities which came into print after 1450, and we began a search for such publications, adding the *Statutes of Verona*, 1475, the *Statutes of Venice*, 1492, and the *Statutes and Decrees of Genoa*, 1498. Such background was fitting for the acquisition of a set of Spanish laws, *Las Pragmaticas*, 1503, edited by Juan Ramirez, and containing the first laws for governing a Spanish colony in America.

Books were not adequate to James Ford Bell's ambitions to find early commercial records, for such records are full of individual transactions handled by notaries and customs officials. His hope was to incorporate into the Library records of trade from the Middle Ages—or earlier if possible—through a microfilming program. To this end the Library's staff was doubled in 1957 with the appointment of Vsevolod Slessarev as a research assistant. "Steve" as we called him was an advanced graduate student at the University of Wisconsin, a specialist in late medieval economic history. His assignment with the Library was to locate a city archive in Italy, or several of them, and negotiate arrangements to microfilm records revealing the nature of the trade of that city. With this in mind Steve spent a summer searching the archives of several Italian cities and settled on Lucca as the most promising, initiating there a microfilming project which in the next two years yielded some two hundred reels of film. Steve's departure for a position at the University of Cincinnati in 1961 and Mr. Bell's death that year brought that aspect of the Library's program to an end, and we returned to the primary focus on books, maps, and manuscripts which could be acquired and used in their original condition.

And so we discovered a flourishing literature of economics, and bundles of laws which sought to order and encourage the commerce of Western European nations, and together they contributed to the bulk that gave value to the Library as a research institution, while the more spectacular voyage literature gave it visibility in the more traditional areas of collecting.

In all of this there was agreement between Mr. Bell and the University Library Administration that the University would buy the less expensive items and he would purchase the materials that could not readily be justified as a University expenditure. As a Regent of the University he understood its finances. There was no written agreement, nor was there a specific financial watershed between the two parties, but good faith and good will were relied upon and they did not fail. There was a large pamphlet literature dealing with economic matters in France and England to which the University had a strong commitment within its collecting traditions. To these it was natural enough to add Dutch materials, since both nations encountered competition from the Dutch in every aspect of overseas trade. The large number of incoming laws, decrees, regulations, etc. were logical University acquisitions, supplementing a fair amount of such material in the Law Library. In no instance was there to be duplication with materials already in any of the University's libraries.

And while such items arrived on an almost daily basis, there were frequent acquisitions of the spectacular sort. While never thinking of the Library as a major map collection, it was natural to add maps which reflected commercial situations and knowledge. Among these were Albino de Canepa's portolan chart made in Genoa, 1489, reaching from the mystical Antillia in the Atlantic to the Black Sea in the east where Genoese trading stations were identified with Genoese flags; the Atlantic chart of Jorge Reinel, ca. 1534, showing Portugal's South Atlantic imperial aspirations with coasts of Africa and Brazil brilliantly displayed; the 1643 map of New France by Jean Boisseau showing French penetration along the Great Lakes as far as Lake Huron; a section of a planisphere from about 1450 showing much of Africa and the Mediterranean Sea; an engraved world map by Oronce Finé, 1531, showing the new discoveries to that time in a double cordiform projection. But in spite of such finds, the main quest was always for texts—the printed book or the manuscript recording Europe's advance into the outer world, for that was the story the Library was designed to tell.

There was some impatience on Mr. Bell's part to put these materials to work telling that story to a modern audience, interpreting these beginnings for our time. Perhaps it was the merchant in him at work here—and he always said that was his profession—for he knew the nucleus was expanding and was capable of teaching history to a general audience and of providing an opportunity for in-depth research by professional scholars. But how could we attract the attention of these diverse groups? First we must tell the world (including more booksellers) who we were and what was the nature of the library we were building.

In 1950 the James Ford Bell Collection had been handsomely described in a catalog prepared by Frank Walter, Director of Libraries at the University of Minnesota, and Virginia Doneghy, a senior member of the Catalog Department. Published by the University of Minnesota Press, this catalog was done in exquisite bibliographical detail in the manner of the John Carter Brown and E.D. Church libraries of Americana. It had taken years to compile and included 163 items. Time precluded our following that pattern. In the years between 1950 and the dedication of the Library the collection had grown by 437 items, and after its installation at the University that growth accelerated sharply. We wanted to make this growth known, and the vehicle decided upon was a published *List of Additions, 1951-1954*, a chronological list with brief annotations, published by the University of Minnesota Press. A subsequent *List of Additions* covered the 1955-1959 period, and two additional *Lists* noted acquisitions through 1969. Anyone who was interested could find out about the progress of the Library.

But for general readers there had to be something more colorful, more readable. A brochure series was begun, the first of them issued in 1955 titled *Antillia and America*, featuring reproductions of the 1424 Nautical Chart and the Waldseemüller Globe Gores. Beautifully designed by Jane McCarthy at the University of Minnesota Press and finely printed at North Central Publishing Company, this and subsequent brochures were freely distributed and they began to gather an audience for the Library.

These were rather brief publications, attuned to serious readers, but not particularly to the scholarly community. Something else was needed for them. We began in 1955 with a simple translation by a visiting professor, Sergio Pacifici, of an Italian newsletter purporting to be a letter from the King of Portugal to the King of Spain announcing the success of Portugal's early voyages to India. It was hoped that this translation of an extremely rare text from 1505 would show our new eastern emphasis. Again, high quality design and production were featured as this was envisioned as the first of a series which would attract both scholars and collectors of beautiful books. Recruiting authors for this annual series was not easy. The Library had not yet earned a reputation among scholars, so it was local professors who were sufficiently curious about the Library to stop in and ask questions who were the earliest authors. Professor Alvin Prottengeier of the German Department translated the German newsletter of 1505 defining the route to India. We titled it *From Lisbon to Calicut*. Professor Mark Graubard from the Physics Department—a maker of navigational instruments—was induced to translate an account of a voyage to the coast of South America from about 1511, and we called the resulting volume *Tidings out of Brazil*.

These small and elegant collectors' items had the desired effect. Scholars learned of them and came forward to express their interest: Donald Weinstein from the University of Iowa, Francis Rogers from Harvard, Charles Nowell from the University of Illinois, Hildegard Johnson from Macalester College. Professor Rogers would write many years later—in 1977—that he and others in the Boston area "sensed something new was going on beyond the western horizon," and that they learned of it in greater detail "through a brilliantly conceived set of publications designed to let them know in most enjoyable fashion what the Bell Library was all about." Needless to say Professor Rogers became one of the Library's great scholarly friends, and he was not alone among the apostles who told the world about this Library.

There was one more avenue to the world that James Ford Bell thought needed exploring. Could we begin to tell the total story of European commercial expansion from the books and manuscripts we had and were acquiring? That is a very large story indeed, and we were still in our nucleus phase as libraries go. It seemed best to tell parts of the story as reflected in current acquisitions, and to do it annually, with one eye on the newspapers to show how present events and the past are closely related. Mr. J. Cameron Thomson, a friend of Mr. Bell and a friend of the Library, once advised us, "if it doesn't relate to the morning news nobody will read it." Having that in mind, along with our urge to reach a larger audience, we brought *The Merchant Explorer* into existence in May, 1961.

James Ford Bell and I met for the last time two days before he died. *The Merchant Explorer* had just come off the press. It was Friday, and late in the afternoon I took a copy to him at the hospital. We talked about it as a messenger that would go out annually to the Library's friends and to those we hoped would become its friends. As always, he liked beginnings, and here in his last days was the start of a new program for the Library. There have been many more beginnings since May, 1961. The Associates organized, the James Ford Bell Lectures started, courses taught, essay awards given, conferences held. But the substance of these reflect those years of beginnings, and they testify to the need always for new beginnings, new ideas, new energies to fulfill the dream that this Library will "someday take its place with others both in the extent and in the values it offers."

THE DESIGN OF THE PRESENT BOOK FOLLOWS THE DESIGN OF *BOOK COLLECTING AND SCHOLARSHIP*, PUBLISHED IN 1954 TO CELEBRATE THE DEDICATION OF THE JAMES FORD BELL LIBRARY AT THE UNIVERSITY OF MINNESOTA. THE EARLY BOOK WAS DESIGNED BY JANE MCCARTHY OF THE UNIVERSITY OF MINNESOTA PRESS, THE FIRST OF MANY FINE PUBLICATIONS FOR THE LIBRARY. THE BOOK WAS PRINTED AT LUND PRESS AND BOUND AT A.J. DAHL COMPANY. THIS 1993 IMITATION OF IT WAS COMPUTER FORMATTED BY BRIAN HANSON. THE PRODUCTION WAS SUPERVISED BY IRV KREIDBERG; THE TEXT WAS EDITED BY CAROL URNESS. THE BOOK WAS PRINTED BY VIKING PRESS AND BOUND BY MIDWEST EDITIONS.